ere she was, standing on the doormat, dripping from the rain. With h
re entered the cold breath of autumn, a frisson that traversed
se and urged us toward the warmth of the fireplace. Her gown sho
the light of the entrance and her bright-coloured shoes looked lik
nges soaked in water. Her hair lay haphazardly, on her temples, l
droplets of water escape helter-skelter, forming languishing tears
cheeks. Her breathing showed that she had been running. But I h
eeling that it wasn't to seek shelter from the rain. No — she had
share a great joy more quickly, as if she sensed instinctively tha

t someone else could easily have played my part in the tableau.
us was finding the words to express to the fullest exactly what
hed to share. Perhaps in her excitement, far too many came to her mi
d then, a ray of sunshine burst through the clouds and suddenly,
ughter cried: "Daddy, I'm in love!" There she was, standing on
ormat, dripping from the rain. With her, there entered the cold breath
tumn, a frisson that traversed the house and urged us toward
rmth of the fireplace. Her gown shone in the light of the entrance a

ere she was, standing on the doormat, dripping from the rain. With
re entered the cold breath of autumn, a frisson that traversed the ho
d urged us toward the warmth of the fireplace. Her gown shone in
t of the entrance and her bright-coloured shoes looked liked spon
aked in water. Her hair lay haphazardly, on her temples, letting drop
water escape helter-skelter, forming languishing tears on her chee

st through the clouds and suddenly, my daughter cried: "Daddy, I'r
e!" There she was, standing on the doormat, dripping from the r
ith her, there entered the cold breath of autumn, a frisson that t
sed the house and urged us toward the warmth of the fireplace.
n shone in the light of the entrance and her bright-coloured sh

True
Happiness

This book belongs to

Published by:
Modus Vivendi Publishing Inc.
3859, Laurentian Autoroute
Laval, Quebec
Canada H7L 3H7
or
2565 Broadway, Suite 161
New York, New York 10025

Graphic Design: Marc Alain
Translation: Brenda O'Brien
Photo Credits:
Cover 1: ©SuperStock; Cover 4: ©Christie's Images/SuperStock
Page 1, 2 and 48: ©Christie's Images/SuperStock

Legal Deposit: 2nd Quarter, 2000
National Library of Canada
Cataloguing in Publication Data
Desbois, Hervé
    True happiness
    (Heartfelt series)
    Translation of: Simple bonheur
    ISBN 2-89523-021-8
    1. Happiness. 2. Happiness - Pictorial works.
    I. Title. II. Series.
BF575.H27D4713 2000   152.4'2   C00-940561-5

Canadä We acknowledge the support of the Government of Canada through the
Book Publishing Industry Development Program for our publishing activities.

True
Happiness

HERVÉ DESBOIS

MV PUBLISHING

"Happiness escapes whomever seeks it."

French proverb

What can be said of happiness? Can it still exist in a modern and materialistic society? This book offers no magic answers — instead, it speaks of happiness simply and directly. Happiness can be easy to find. It comes, it goes, as capricious as the wind, as soft as a caress, as energizing as the springtime sunshine; it comes into our lives when we least expect it, it escapes us when we most want it. And yet, it can be genuinely present, though we refuse to recognize it.

Is life nothing more than a long quest for happiness? Are each of our actions motivated by this single quest, even though it may be unconscious? At times, do we confuse pleasure with happiness? True happiness, complete happiness, is something that is shared.

Happiness is never calculated, it never occurs without a reason. No formula can conjure happiness from the mystery of our existence. There is nothing mathematical or logical in this wonderful state of being. No chemical formula can create it. Happiness belongs to the soul, it is intangible. And though we can share it with others, though others can create it in our lives, like a seed, it depends totally and absolutely on our nurturing.

"Humans carry in them the seeds of all happiness and all misfortune."

Sophocles
Greek philosopher

The Aura of Happiness

On an unknown sidewalk
The perfume of a stranger
Is carried on a smile
And suddenly nothing is the same

Jading or intoxicating
It inhabits us for a moment
And we are magically happy
No reason, no rhyme

Happiness is a fragile occurrence
That happens along our path
When we seek it least
It chooses to embrace us

Its magic encircles us
We seek to grasp it
We seek to cling to it
We seek to capture it

But it comes and goes
Light as a breeze
Strong as the most passionate of loves
Able to inhabit and captivate us

Happiness roams free
To us the task of finding it

And suddenly, it is there
It is a part of our lives

© Leslie Braddock/SuperStock

"In each of our lives, there are so many things that can make us happy."

Arthur Rubinstein

There are many, many small sources of happiness, and they can be multiplied time and time again. Particular moments, though sometimes brief, can create a state of absolute serenity. If we can learn to recognize such moments, we can enjoy them to the fullest when they occur. I have fond memories of summer evenings, when I was a child. After a full day of running and playing with my friends, it was time to go home. The sun was setting, shooting vibrant red into the cool blue of the sky. Night was falling softly, and the heat of the day was yielding its embrace to a soft and enveloping breeze.

This was the time Mother chose to cut the green beans she'd bought at the local farmers' market. Comfortably and quietly seated on a chair in the front yard, she peeled bright green pods into a newspaper laid on her knees. "Plop, plop, plop." The beans dropped one by one into a bowl of ice-cold water at her feet. I used to watch her, sitting on the last step of the porch. All the day's excitement seemed to fade away in the shadow of her calm and quieting gestures.

"Would you like to help me?"

"Only if I can peel them like I want to."

My mother knew what my bean peeling ritual was. But she always pretended to be surprised.

"And how would that be?"

Wordlessly, I would run into the house and come back with a pair of scissors. Then I would sit beside my mother and begin to peel the beans, using my scissors slowly and precisely.

"What are you doing? Are you silly? Nobody uses scissors to peel beans."

There was never the slightest note of impatience or displeasure in my mother's voice, only a hint of amusement and a hint that she was willing to play my game.

And the short while we spent together, in the silence of nightfall, I was filled with a simple and inexplicable happiness. It was as if the calm of a world ready to sleep, coupled with my mother's tenderness, filled my very being with a sense of love. I felt so serene, so wonderfully calm that my being seemed to transcend my body. These small moment of happiness I enjoyed without ever questioning their existence. They were there, they existed for me and for my mother, for anyone willing to see them. I had but to embrace them.

"How about a bean salad?"

"If that's what you'd like, my dear boy."

Mom's bean salad — what joy, what happiness!

"Happiness is always accessible for those willing to savour it."

François de La Rochefoucauld
1613-1680, French author

Happiness and Creativity

"There are only two ingredients for happiness: believing and loving."

Charles Nodier, French author

You've just given the last brush stroke to your latest painting, something you've been working on for weeks; you experience a feeling of tremendous satisfaction as you reread the report you're about to hand in to your boss; at long last, you've found the words to finish the poem that you've had in the back of your mind for so long; you've succeeded in making one of your fondest dreams come true, after hours and hours of patient and tireless work. Creativity, regardless of its kind, is an endless source of happiness.

However, a few mean-spirited people will tell you that they too could have done as much, just as well. Don't let them discourage you. Savour your happiness. Let no one spoil it. You are the person who has accomplished what you originally set out to do. They merely talk about their dreams.

"Look within yourself for the answer to your questions. Refuse the negative influence of those around you: refuse their thoughts, refuse their words."

Eileen Caddy

The following is a "creation" loved by young and old. One of my mother's recipes, probably handed down to her by her own mother, and probably one that she will hand down.

The joy of springtime, the sound of birds, trees growing green and coming to live again, the beauty of cherry blossom time! Huge cherries, juicy and oh! so sweet. And the delicious prospect of "Cherry Clafoutis".

Cherry Clafoutis

To serve approximately four people, you need:

- 350 grams/1½ cup of cherries
- 100 grams/1 cup of flour
- 150 grams/¾ cup of sugar (less if you use fructose)
- 3 eggs
- 1 large glass of milk (more or less)
- a pinch of salt

Begin by washing and removing the stalks from the cherries. Stone them, especially if you have young children or if you want to enjoy your dessert without having to worry about pits. However, note that stoning the cherries removes a bit of their flavour. Place the cherries in the bottom of a buttered dish (a pie or gratin dish).

In a large bowl, mix the flour, the sugar and the salt; fold in the whole eggs, then add the lukewarm milk. The mixture should resemble a very thick pancake mix. Pour the mixture over the cherries and place in a hot oven (approximately 350°F, depending on the oven type); bake for 45 minutes.

Eat cold or lukewarm. Be warned: you may regret not having made a larger quantity!

"The happiest man is he who has spread the most happiness to those around him."

Denis Diderot, French author and philosopher

"Happiness lies not in wealth, but in how you choose to use it."

Miguel de Cervantes, Spanish author

"Most humans set conditions for happiness. But we find happiness only when we cease to set conditions."

A. Rubinstein

"In happiness, even among the best of us, there is always a gentle arrogance daring others to do as much."

Victor Hugo, French author

"Happiness is like a watch: the less complicated it is, the easier it is to read."

Chamfort, French author

"Pleasure is merely happiness concentrated in one particular part of our bodies. True happiness, genuine happiness, complete happiness is a state of well-being that permeates our souls."

Joseph Joubert, French moralist

"It is the soul that makes us good or evil, that makes us happy or unhappy, rich or poor."

Edmund Spenser, British poet

"What cowardice to be discouraged by the happiness of others, to be overwhelmed by their good fortune."

Montesquieu, French author

My Sunshine

When the dawn emerges from the night
It is you I see
When I emerge from the silence of the dark
It is you I see
You are like a river
That flows through my dreams
Without you, where would I find light?

When the city veils your smile
It is you I look for
When life batters me and steals my sighs
It is you I look for
You are a fortress
That guards and protects me
Without you, where is my shelter, my refuge?

Let me lay down and sleep
In the shadow of your eyes
When I am exhausted by the journey of time
As it passes so swiftly and so indifferently

I treasure the sight
Of the smile on your lips
You are the brilliant light
Of the sun in my skies

You, my love, my happiness

> **"The sweetest kind of happiness is the happiness we share."**
>
> Jacques Delille, French poet

There she was, standing on the doormat, dripping from the rain. With her, there entered the cold breath of autumn, a frisson that traversed the house and urged us toward the warmth of the fireplace. Her gown shone in the light of the entrance and her bright-coloured shoes looked liked sponges soaked in water. Her hair lay haphazardly on her temples, letting droplets of water escape helter-skelter, forming languishing tears on her cheeks.

Her breathing showed that she had been running. But I had a feeling that it wasn't to seek shelter from the rain. No — she had run to share a great joy more quickly, as if she sensed instinctively that a shared happiness is a doubled happiness, one that regenerates itself endlessly.

There she was, trembling in her wet clothing. Yet she was radiant. In her eyes was a new fire, one I had never seen before, and all of the torrents from heaven had not succeeded in dimming the sunshine that seemed to emanate from her.

This special moment — one that seemed to contain in it the very essence of life — I had no wish to spoil with mere words. I left to her the decision to speak if she so wished.

And although she remained silent, her eyes, her smile and everything that radiated from her spoke volumes. Seated in the living room armchair, my book open but unread on my knees, I sat contemplating her, as if she were an apparition. I was in no hurry. I had the wonderful feeling of experiencing a moment that could transcend time, a magical moment, one I would never fully understand. An energizing moment as invisible and as present as the wind.

Her need to confide in me was increasingly perceptible. But I knew that someone else could easily have played my part in the tableau. Her focus was finding the words to express to the fullest exactly what she wished to share. Perhaps in her excitement, far too many came to her mind.

And then, a ray of sunshine burst through the clouds and suddenly, my daughter cried:

"Daddy, I'm in love!"

Happiness can be contagious. Be quick to pass it on to others.

"**Plant the seeds of happiness in your neighbour's field — you will be astonished to see what the wind will carry to yours.**"

Juliette St-Gelais

What do we sow? Good humour or bad news? And what to think about the rumours circulated on one person or another? We've all listened to them attentively and eventually, we've all repeated a few of them. Is this really the way to spread happiness or to attract it?

Following is a story that, while it isn't new, still proves incontrovertibly that it is better "to count to ten" before making a reckless statement.

One day someone came to Socrates, the eminent Greek philosopher of Antiquity, and said:

"Do you know what I have just found out about your friend?"

"One moment," said Socrates. "Before you tell me, I would like you to submit to the test of the three filters."

"The three filters?"

"Yes," said Socrates. "Before telling all manner of tales about others, it is wise to take the time to filter what you say. This is the test of the three filters. The first filter is truth. Have you verified that what you are about to tell me is true?"

"No. It is simply something I have overheard."

"Very well. So you cannot be sure that it is true. Now let us move on to the second filter: goodness. Are you about to tell me something good about the person?"

"No. On the contrary."

"So," continued Socrates, "you want to tell me something bad about this person and you are not sure that what you are telling me is true. You may yet pass the test. Now comes the filter called usefulness. Is what

you have to say about my friend something that will be useful to me?"

"No. Not really."

"So," added Socrates, "if what you have to say is neither true, nor good, nor useful, why say it?"

♣

Alone on a desert island, only you and I... The eternal dream of Southern oceans, blue waters and endless sandy beaches. Happiness!

May I suggest you explore another kind of island, more affordable and much more easily accessible: "Floating Islands" for the Robinson Crusoes among us, whether male or female.

Custard

- 1/2 litre/3³/4 cup of milk
- 1 small pinch of salt
- 4 or 5 egg yolks
- 1 packet of vanilla-flavoured sugar
- 100 g/1/2 cup of powered sugar

Boil the milk with the salt and vanilla-flavoured sugar. In a bowl, mix together the egg yolks and the sugar (set aside the egg whites) until the mixture turns white. Off the burner, add the boiling milk to the mixture.

Pour into a clean saucepan. Set over low heat and stir thoroughly, scraping the bottom of the saucepan. Continue stirring until the cream mixture thickens and coats a spoon. Remove from the burner before the mixture boils. Pour the cream into a dish and let cool.

Floating Islands

Boil a small quantity of salted water. Beat the egg whites until they are stiff. When the water is boiling, drop heaping spoonfuls of the egg white mixture into it. Place the egg white islands on the sea of custard. Savour. Close your eyes, enjoy your own special island adventure.

"Happiness is often the only thing that we can give without truly possessing it; and when we give it, we instantly acquire it."

Voltaire, French author

"A love remembered is much like love itself — it is a special form of happiness."

Goethe, German author and scholar

"No happiness comes without a few clouds."

French proverb

"Happiness is the delicate balance between what we are and what we have."

Anonymous

"Happiness is the ability to continue wanting what you already have."

Saint Augustine, French bishop

"As you awake in the morning, remember how precious is the privilege to live, to breathe, to be happy."

Marcus Aurelius, Roman emperor

"Happiness is a wonderful commodity: the more you give, the more you get."

Suzanne Curchod

"Men are who they are because of their personalities, they are happy because of their actions, or vice versa."

Aristotle, Greek philosopher

Shared Happiness

As I remember our Sundays
Two bodies and two souls intertwined
Filled with love and worry-free
Seeing our dreams come true
I am inhabited by hidden happiness
The gentle breezes of endless summers
I am mesmerized by your smiling face
As I awake in the light of dawn

When our contentment begins to fade
As the sun sometimes slips behind the clouds
We reiterate our words of love
And our happiness is renewed

As time continues to slip by
Our hands continue to reach out
In our childlike hearts and our shining eyes
Is the precious innocence of youth

We chose each other for the unseen
The beauty that even time cannot alter
The sparkling light in our respective souls
The wondrous experience of shared happiness

> "The greatest key to happiness is being happy with yourself."

Fontenelle

George used to be a sailor. With his blond hair and a face sculpted by the high winds, he resembled a Viking warrior from the legends of centuries long past. His bushy beard and shiny blue eyes were the finishing touches to a classical profile. He had sailed on all of the world's oceans, drunk in taverns in every port, frequented the loose women and ruffians typical of the murky circles of the underworld. He had fought more than one enemy, real or imagined — over a girl, over a drink, over nothing at all. At times, his stories froze my blood. But I could believe what he said was true, just by looking into his eyes, into the remnants of his anger, his shame, his hate.

When I met George, his life as a sailor was over. He had sailed into port for good. George had used the sea to flee and to forget an unhappy childhood. He believed that he could find peace of mind by leaving his memories far, far behind, that he could find happiness in travel and adventure. Despite the many years he spent on all of the planet's waters, he failed to find what he was searching for so desperately. In his eyes was the sadness of those who have looked much too hard, finding only fleeting pleasures, easily consumed and soon forgotten. George lived with disappointed hopes and useless memories. And then the inevitable occurred; one day, he decided to leave again. To set sail again. He shared nothing of his destination nor of his projects, if he had any.

"What can I say... I'm a sailor and I don't take to dry docks. In the end, I am searching for my true self. And as long as I don't know why I've been put here on earth, I will never be happy."

Many years passed before I encountered George again. I had had absolutely no news of him. Then one day, like a scene in a movie, George reappeared. He dropped by, impulsively, without any warning. I almost didn't recognize him. Yet he had changed very little: the same blond hair, the same beard, though maybe a little tidier now. But his face looked younger and in his eyes, I could see Life. We greeted each other warmly, hugging and hastily wiping away a tear or two. Although we were understandibly happy to see each other, our outpouring of emotion was something unusual.

"George, you've changed. I'm so happy to see you. How are you?"

"Oh, my dear old friend, if you only knew! I began to discover my true self when I stopped being selfish. I discovered that I had a lot of love to give to others. It had always been there, hidden away deep inside me. You know, when I set out to find happiness, my own happiness, I found God! And that is what made me happier than I've ever been."

"On life's highways and byways, we seek happiness. But happiness is with us, in the here and now, wherever we may be."

Horace, Latin poet

When is the time to be happy?

"If we are not happy now, today, which day will bring us happiness?"

Hsun-Tzu

Fond memories are happiness held in reserve. We can unearth them from our memory as often as we want, without ever exhausting the happiness they bring with them. At times, it is enough simply to think of a happy memory and it succeeds in bringing a smile to our face on an otherwise very dreary morning.

Happy memories can help us create a more beautiful present, especially if they remind us that we once believed in our dreams, if they show us that we can believe in them once again.

Plunge your soul into your happy memories, just as plants plunge their roots into the nurturing earth, in search of newfound energy to make them as strong and as vibrant as possible.

"Do not wait for events to unfold as you wish them to unfold. Decide to want what occurs... and you will be happy."

Epictetus, Stoic philosopher, 1st century B.C.

The following is one of the many recipes that made my childhood an extremely happy time. My mother would make this dish in the fall or winter, when she didn't have a lot of time to prepare our meal, or when she simply wanted to please us. She called it a "Short-and-Sweet", precisely because it could be made in no time at all. But beware, it is very nouri-

shing and it makes the house smell wonderful! It's an amazing dessert, a meal in itself. My mother used to begin by serving us soup — and the promise of her "Short-and-Sweet" was the very best way to get me to empty my bowl.

Here are the ingredients you need to make enough for four "ogres" or six "tiny tots".

- 120 grams/1 cup of flour
- 250 grams/1¼ cup of sugar or fructose
- 6 eggs
- ½ litre of milk

Separate the egg whites from the yolks and beat the egg whites until they are stiff. When they begin to peak or when you can turn the bowl upside down and the whites don't spill out, they are the right consistency. (If they do spill out, they just weren't ready!) In a separate bowl, mix together the egg yolks and the sugar. Slowly add the cold milk. Next add the flour, little by little, stirring until the mixture is smooth. Gently add the egg whites. Avoid crushing the egg whites; if you do, the preparation will not rise during baking. Pour the mixture into a greased mould.

Bake in a preheated 350°F oven, for approximately 25 minutes; the "Short-and-Sweet" should bake to a nice golden brown. It is done when you can insert a knife and it comes out clean. Eat it fast, the "Short-and-Sweet" waits for no man (or child)!

I hope you enjoy this dish as much as I did as a child and that your culinary experience will be a happy one. I know the "Short-and-Sweet" still makes me happy... especially when I make it for my own children.

"Happiness belongs to those who have the ability to make others happy."

Abbé Delille

"There is no happiness without freedom, and no freedom without courage."

Pericles, Greek politician

"Be content, it is the only true happiness."

Louis-Auguste Commerson

"Happiness is like a perfume, we cannot spread it to others without getting a few drops on ourselves."

Ralph Waldo Emerson
American philosopher and poet

"If you wish to live a happy life, do not exaggerate its misfortunes and do not overlook its joys."

Joseph Joubert, French moralist

"We persist in acting as if comfort and luxury were essential to our existence, yet to be truly happy, we need only find something of passionate interest to us."

Charles Kingsley, British author

"There is more joy in giving than in receiving."

Saint Luke, Apostle

"I call character in a man the resolve to set out in search of happiness."

Stendhal, French author

I am...

I am the loveliest of the lovely
The handsomest of gods
I warm you like the sun
Regardless of the season

I am in the eyes of your beloved
Or in the face of a child
In the smile of a stranger
And in the laughter of lovers

I am everywhere in Nature
In the flowers that you tend
You see me in the azure sky
You feel me in the morning dew

I am in winter's first snowflakes
That dance and twirl in the wind
And in the song of the swalows
A harbinger of spring

I am here, I am elsewhere
I am endless, I am ageless
I am deep in each heart
I am the thousand faces of happiness

"In the happiness of others, I seek my own happiness."

Pierre Corneille, French dramatic poet

"Yes, there can be no doubt that in every formula for happiness there is the idea of merit."

Joseph Joubert, French moralist

"As soon as we recognize that all of us must strive to ensure the happiness of others, we will have overcome our biggest obstacle in life."

Joseph Bonaparte,
King of Spain from 1808 to 1813

"Life is like a rainbow: it takes rain and sunshine to make its colours come to life."

Anonymous

"Do you want to be happy? Travel with two bags: one for giving, the other for receiving."

Goethe, German author and scholar

"Happiness is not a wild plant that grows spontaneously, like the weeds in a garden; it is a delicious fruit, made so only with sustained effort."

Nicolas Restif, 1734-1806,
French author

"Happy is the man who falls to sleep knowing that he has done all that he could do."

Bhagavad-Gita

"I work at being happy: it is the most beautiful of all occupations."

R. Lassus

re she was, standing on the doormat, dripping from the rain. With

e entered the cold breath of autumn, a frisson that traversed the ho

d urged us toward the warmth of the fireplace. Her gown shone in

of the entrance and her bright-coloured shoes looked liked spot

ked in water. Her hair lay haphazardly, on her temples, letting drop

water escape helter-skelter, forming languishing tears on her che

breathing showed that she had been running. But I had a feeling

asn't to seek shelter from the rain. No — she had run to share a

ave played my part in the tableau. Her focus was finding the wor

ress to the fullest exactly what she wished to share. Perhaps in

tement, far too many came to her mind. And then, a ray of suns

t through the clouds and suddenly, my daughter cried: "Daddy, I

e!" There she was, standing on the doormat, dripping from the

th her, there entered the cold breath of autumn, a frisson that trave

house and urged us toward the warmth of the fireplace. Her

ne in the light of the entrance and her bright-coloured shoes lo